M000020644

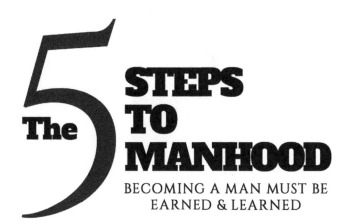

The 5 STEPS TO MANHOOD

BECOMING A MAN MUST BE EARNED & LEARNED

BARON WARREN

To: Mr. Terrell

With the Upmost

Respect sir!

5-22-20

CONTENTS

The 5 Steps to Manhood: Becoming a Man must be Earned and Learned

Copyright © 2020 by Baron Warren. All rights reserved.

No part of this book may be used or reproduced in any manner whatsoever without written permission except in the case of brief quotations embodied in critical articles or reviews.

For Information Contact:
Baron Warren
www.cutsandcoaching.com | www.baronwarren.com

Book and Cover Design | Editing
DHBonner Virtual Solutions, LLC
www.dhbonner.net

ISBN: 978-0-578-63818-8

Printed in The United States of America

*To my beautiful daughters, Alecia & Jordane,
you are my everything! You are the reason I get up every
morning. You are what motivates me to strive for excellence.
I didn't know what it truly meant to be a MAN
until you came into my life.*

*Thank you for always loving me, supporting me,
and encouraging me in every way. This book,
I dedicate to you.*

Love you, girls, forever!
Daddy

AN AMERICAN TRAGEDY

June 2, 2017 is a day that will forever go down in history. This was the day that an American tragedy took place in the city of Detroit, Michigan. What makes this tragedy unique from other horrific events in our nation's history is the fact that no causalities occurred. At least not in the natural sense. No police were called, although a crime had been committed.

No one that was in attendance at this local event even noticed that one of the greatest crimes in America had just taken place. And the most shocking thing is that this particular tragedy is an event that happens every day. What on earth could this be?

I start my day excited about the event that my beautiful daughters and I had been talking about all year long. I had saved my money to rent a limousine for the occasion. My oldest daughter had told her friends about the details of her beautiful black dress with the imitation diamonds that elegantly covered the material of her gown. My youngest daughter had explained to me that her hair must be just right -- flat iron, curls, hair spray, and the perfect hairpin appropriate for a queen – no mistakes could be made.

I, too, am very detailed about my attire, in a custom fit tuxedo-style white suit jacket with black silk pants and a relaxed bowtie that looks like something out of a James Bond movie. Oh, and let me not forget the sophisticated sunglasses that will set me apart from all the others in the room. This is the night that surpasses any other night. I had planned the perfect night on the town with my two beautiful daughters. We were now ready for the event of the year: The DADDY DAUGHTER DANCE!

Now, depending on your geographical location, you may not have heard of such an event, so let me explain. The daddy-daughter dance is an extraordinary event. This is an event where fathers take their daughters out for a night on the town in superb fashion. Not only is this a special time where fathers can spend some unique quality time with their daughters, but it is an opportunity to display a father's love publicly.

At this event, you will be entertained by any and everything that a little girl in a Cinderella movie could dream of. There, the most excellent food is served by pleasant waiters and waitresses. The room is decorated in a way that encourages you to take your daughter by the hand and share a romantic dance that will leave all spectators forever in awe.

The photo booth is ready to snap magical photos that will be placed on the family dining room table or posted immediately on your favorite social media outlet (Facebook, Snapchat, Instagram) for friends and family to share the moment with you. But most importantly, the daddy-daughter dance is an opportunity for a father to show his daughter what a real man looks like.

This event allows fathers to set the bar for his daughter as to how a man should treat a woman. The goal of this event is to carve in every young girl's heart the beauty of a daughter's relationship with her father and how it will set the tone for any and every man that comes in her life moving forward. It has been said that every girl should have a moment like this with her father. It is the experience of a lifetime.

We arrive at the event only to be greeted by all the other fathers and daughters waiting in line to enter one of Detroit's finest banquet halls. To my surprise, we were the only family to arrive in a luxury limousine. This made my daughters feel even more special, and as a father, it made me feel proud that I was able to set my daughters apart from the majority. We enter the ballroom, and the magic began immediately. It felt like something out of a love story. Singing, dancing, laughing filled the room as I dance the night away with my daughters. This night couldn't get any better, and I was confident that this night would remain perfect in every way.

After dancing to at least five songs back to back, it was officially time for me to take a break and rest my legs.

"Girls, daddy is a little tired, I'm going to take a quick break, but don't worry, I will be back soon."

"Okay, Daddy," my girls replied.

I made my way to the closest empty table, and that's when it happened, America's worst tragedy.

As I look across the room, I saw a little girl sitting at the table all alone with a strange look on her face. She kind of had a blank stare and seemed as if she was having an out of body experience. She fumbled around with her fingers as she watched all the girls dance with their fathers. Her eyes welled up as if she wanted to cry but couldn't let it out.

Something was definitely bothering her, and for the life of me, I couldn't just let it go. With caution and concern, I approach the young girl. "Excuse me, young lady, is everything okay?" I asked her.

"Mr. Warren, yes, everything is okay. How are you doing today?"

OMG, how on earth did this young lady know my name? From my recollections, I had never seen this little girl before. She said it with such confidence and certainty that it startled me.

"WOW, how do you know my name? Oh, and by the way, what's your name?"

"Jessica," she replied. "Oh, and I'm friends with your daughters. they told me that you were bringing them here."

"It's such a pleasure to meet you, Ms. Jessica. Thank you for being friends with my daughters. I am happy that we are all here to enjoy this special event," I replied.

As I continue to talk, Jessica interrupted me and said,

"Mr. Warren, would it be possible for us to take a picture together, and maybe after we could dance, sing and laugh?"

Immediately I became startled again. It was a question I wasn't prepared for and, of course, caused some concern. As I prepared a response, I notice that Jessica had an interested look in her eyes.

Her look was filled with hope and pain all at the same time – as if I said the right answer, her life would be forever changed in an extraordinary way. But if I gave the wrong answer, she would enter an area of disappointment that would be beyond my comprehension.

After what I felt like was an extremely long pause, I replied.

"Yes, Ms. Jessica, I would be honored to dance with you, but I must ask, where is your Father?"

Jessica replied, "Mr. Warren, I don't know my father. I have never seen him before."

I replied with such passion and said, "Ms. Jessica, please forgive me. I am so confused. You have never met your father, and you came to the Daddy Daughter Dance all alone?"

With pain and passion in her eyes yet again, she replied, "Yes, Mr. Warren. I did."

Then, with a long deep breath, and maybe the comfort of her knowing she was in a safe environment to share what was heavy on her heart, she took me on a field trip in her world without a father.

She began, "Mr. Warren, I have heard stories about girls spending time with their dad, but not me.

I have heard that dads help the daughters with their homework, not me. I heard that dads walk their daughter to school, but not me. I heard that dads treat our moms nice, but not me. I have always heard that dads love daughters in a special way, but not me.

What's wrong with me, Mr. Warren?" she asked.

As my heart began to race so fast as if it was about to jump out of my chest, I respectfully said, "Ms. Jessica, thank you for sharing such personal details with me. May I ask, why did you decide to come to the Daddy Daughter Dance alone?"

She replied, "Mr. Warren, I was told that all of my friends would be here. I was told there would be singing, dancing and laughing all night long. I read the flyer, and it said that every young lady should attend this event. The flyer said that every little girl should be treated like a queen. Mr. Warren, after I heard all these things and read the flyer, I just didn't want to miss the party."

As her head began to sink in her chest, and her eyes began to gaze at the floor, she ended her statement with these words. "Mr. Warren, why isn't my daddy here? Where is he? What's wrong with me?"

Fighting back a storm of tears that were beginning to fill up in my soul, I began to say these words.

"Ms. Jessica, there is nothing wrong with you. You have done nothing wrong but have done everything right. Because you had the courage to attend an event that some would say you were disqualified for, you have displayed an enormous amount of strength. You have proven that there is no task too great for a woman with a desire to be honored in this unique way. Today, Ms. Jessica, I am honored to be in your presence, and it would be a pleasure to invite you to share this moment with me and my daughters. Would that be okay?"

Ms. Jessica looked at me as if she had known me her whole life. Her eyes began to clear and shine bright. The smile that covered her face was for all to see and was dangerously contagious. Something changed in Ms. Jessica when she stood up and embraced me with the sincerest hug I have ever received in my life.

I knew that it was by divine order that we had met. I also knew that it was now my responsibility to show Ms. Jessica what a real man looks like. I took Ms. Jessica by the hand, walked her over to my daughters, and the three of us danced the night away.

Because of the type of man that I am, I took it upon myself to do some investigating of my own. I began to communicate with Ms. Jessica's mom to learn more about their situation. Without a hint of hesitation, I was informed by Ms. Jessica's mom that her father lives right down the street from where they stay. Not only has he not interacted with Ms. Jessica, but he has purposely avoided her and avoided his responsibilities as a father. Ms. Jessica attended the dance alone, and her father lives right down the street.

To all that have taken the time to read this book, this is what I call an American tragedy! Right now, as I type these words, there is another little girl at the daddy-daughter dance all alone.

Right now, there is a little boy thinking about joining a street gang with the expectation to gain a sense of acceptance, love, and achievement. Right now, there is a little girl thinking about gaining the love and affection from a boy because her father wasn't in her life to show her what real loves look like from a real man. Right now, there is a young man who has decided on being a criminal, a career path with the certainty that he will enter in and out of the walls of the prison system for many years to come. Right now, there are millions of males that have no idea what it means to be a real man because no one has never shown them. Right now, there are millions of males that have fathered children, yet have not been properly equipped on how to function as a father. Right now, there are millions of males that are in a relationship, married, or with a girlfriend and have no idea about the role as the head of the home.

Right now, there are millions of single mothers raising children alone because the male has not made raising his children a priority and has left the mother to do it all alone. Right now, there are millions of males walking the earth that have no clue how to be a man.

Which brings me to my purpose for writing this book.

Come take a journey with me as I share my personal story

and the five steps that I believe every male must make in order to earn the right to be called a man. It is my prayer that all who read find clarity on the role that all men have as the Pastor, Protector, and Provider of their home.

Let the journey begin!

WHO'S THE MAN?

It is just another cold, bitter day on the mean streets of Detroit. This is the time of the year when the weatherman is reporting a temperature below o degrees all month long. Although the atmosphere remains at record-breaking lows, this does not change the business of the day.

The young men on the street corners, wrapped in warm clothes as they position themselves for all incoming clientele. Day or night, the corner never stops. There is a product that is a desperate need for all that dare to entertain its evil wonders.

In between every business transaction, you may hear the words to your favorite rap song recited for all to hear — word for word, with no errors between each breath. The delivery is as perfect as the artist that created the original lyrics. The momentum of the atmosphere has a way of capturing you and helping you forget about the negative temperatures that continue to breeze by. After a flawless effort, you will then hear the cheers of your peers.

"That was sweet, bro. You are the Man!"

After multiple sessions of rapping and rhyming, it is now time to get back to business. Client after client, sale after sale, dollar after dollar. All day long, until the last customer was served.

After a long day of hustling, it is now time to count the earnings. "How much did you make, bro?" says the young guy to his business partner.

"I made about $300, how about you?" he replied.

"I made $700 today," says the more seasoned youngster as he proudly counts his cash in front of the rookie.

"WOW! $700 in one day? You are the MAN!" he says with admiration for the street veteran.

Just another day in the city as I take the ride to school with the man that raised me since birth. Although not my biological father, he has continued to function in that position since the day of my earliest memory. "Remember, son, it's important that you go to school and get an education so you can get a good job."

He would often say, "a good education will open up many doors for you. If you get a good one, you will be marketable, and then the sky's the limit. Another option is to learn a trade so you can start your own business just like I did. Being self-employed is a great feeling and you will always love what you do. Either way, you will be able to take care of your family, and you will be the man!" says my father figure.

It seems like similar words were quoted to me each and every day as I rode to school with the man that proudly took accountability for me and my mother's other two children.

He was proud to lead this family.
He was proud to own his own business.
He delighted in this position every day.

He truly believed that there was no other way to operate. And it was his belief; this was the definition of a real man. "Have a good day, pops," I would strangely say as I showed respect for him as my stepfather, but always trying to remain loyal to my biological father. "Seems like forever since the last time I seen him," I would often wonder. "How could this be when he lives about 20–30 minutes away?" a constant question that floats through my mind as the days, weeks, and sometimes years go by without me seeing my real dad.

As I enter the school building, I'm greeted daily by the staff members who are proudly on-post. "Good morning, Mr. Warren, and pull those pants up, sir," says my basketball coach.

Every time I see him, he is always well put together like something out of the military. Clean haircut, shirt tucked in, bold, confident voice, and always moving with a purpose. "I got you, coach," I would often reply. "I don't want any problems. You're the man!" I would sometimes say in a very sarcastic tone.

The days are long here at school. I really don't want to be here, and at this season of my life, I don't even feel that school is necessary. I mean, what's the point? "I can't wait to graduate so I can finally do what I want to do. No rules. No teachers. No worries," a thought that crossed my mind at least once a day during those academic years.

As the clock tick-tocks, I find it comical that my classmate James always sits at the front of the class. James is known to be a square, nerd, or teacher's pet. He is always dressed neat, well-spoken, polite to the teachers, and always gets good grades.

"James, you're such a fine young man!" My math teacher would publicly say. A smug look from all the other not-so-well-groomed boys would be made as a little jealousy ran deep in our spirits.

RING! RING! 3:15 pm, the best time of the day. The bell has rung, and school is officially over. YES! It was very common to race home and get to the top priority of the day: video games, talking on the phone, searching for girls, and sleep. I mean, at 16 years old, what could be more important?

During this time of the year, nighttime falls rather quickly. 5 pm is starting to look more and more like midnight. Although I have experienced this time of the year many times, as well as the events of the day, something is strange about today's experience. I can feel something in the air.

With a soft heart and concerned demeanor for the things to

come, my precious mother calls me in the living room to prepare me for the unthinkable. "Son, I have some bad news to tell you. One of your closest friends has been shot and killed."

Time literally stops, and my mind begins to race. With the unique feeling of being devastated, as well as prepared, considering I lost several other loved ones to gun violence, my demeanor is of hurt, pain, and rage.

As I open the door to catch my breath, I am not only greeted by an intensely cold breeze but also a gathering of the "who's who" of the neighborhood. This is standard procedure, or some would even call it tradition when someone is killed in the community. It is now time to gather at the location of the incident and discuss what we believe has taken place.

One by one, all the neighbors come out of their home to try to get a look at his body laid on the icy cold pavement while surrounded by Detroit's police and homicide tape. "What happened to him?" many of the neighbors, both young and old, would ask. "Who would do such a thing to someone so young?" another neighbor would say. Without any hesitation, one of my peers yells out, "It's okay. He died like a man!"

ARE YOU A MAN?

Throughout my life, I have come across a wide variety of males in search of the answer to this singular question. What does it mean to be a real man? My life's journey has brought me to this certain conclusion, and the basis for this book. Are you ready? Here it is:

I was born a MALE, but I must
earn the right to be called a MAN.

Although there were many other males that came into my life, it is vital for you to see a few different types and what they represented. For starters, you must understand that being a man has nothing to do with your age. YOU DO NOT BECOME A MAN ON YOUR 18th BIRTHDAY! You become legal in the eyes of the government, but you have not earned the right to call yourself a man. You become a man the moment you decide to live a life of integrity! That's it!

Let's look at the chart and compare:

What Does Not Make You a Man:

- Your 18th birthday
- Having a child
- Using/selling drugs
- Learning your favorite rap song
- Going to prison
- Being a skilled fighter
- Multiple girlfriends
- Dying proudly in the streets

What Does Make You a Man:

- Deciding to live a life of integrity at any age
- Being an active and responsible father
- Learning a skill and being legally employed
- Making education a priority
- Respecting the law and authority figures
- Protecting yourself and your family when called upon
- Being faithful and committed to one woman
- Maximizing your potential and leaving a legacy for your family

As a young male growing up in a tough inner-city, I was able to experience the difference between being male versus being a man firsthand, from my peers wasting their potential selling poison to the masses by selling drugs. Or, how about my basketball coach who regularly gave me a daily example of what strength, professionalism, and integrity looked like. How about the two males that played a vital role in my depiction of what it means to be a responsible father.

The man that some would call my stepfather, who took on the role and responsibility of raising me. Being held accountable for my livelihood and making it a priority to be a positive influence. While the man who gave me natural life never made it a priority to be present.

WHO'S THE MAN?

Finally, to my friend who I miss dearly, that called the streets his home, who was raised by the influence of the neighborhood street veterans — to die on the corner, on a cold, bitter day at the age of 16 for a senseless, unknown reason is not the definition of manhood.

Although tragic, this way of dying should not be cause for celebration or glorification. My peers on the corner, my dear friend that lost his life — and as I write these pages — my dear father, never graduated from male-hood to manhood. The question is, have you?

40-YEAR-OLD BOY VS 12-YEAR-OLD MAN

As a national speaker and personal development coach, there is one thing that always disturbs me during my travels. Frequently, I get a call from a staff member of a correctional facility (prison) to come and speak to the incarcerated population. This is something I am very passionate about, and I eagerly accept the opportunity. But each time I go, the same frustrating experience occurs.

The staff member meets me at a gate and walks me through the prison to meet the population. Typically, we walk the prison yard or the housing unit, and this is what I see: 20-year-old, 30-year-old, 40-year-old, 50-year-old, even 60-year-old boys. Or should I say, males!

This has got to be one of the most frustrating times in my career. I see a bunch of males that are laughing, joking, complaining, upset, using profanity, and not taking their situation seriously.

Now, don't get me wrong, in my experience, I have also met a lot of MEN that are interested in reentering society with a new attitude and a sincere heart to change for the better. But honestly, the vast majority I meet are not. That being said, in my opinion, although they may have reached the legal age as to be recognized as an adult, they still haven't earned the right to be called a man. They are a 40-year-old male/boy!

What's interesting about this example is that I have a similar experience in the public school setting. Oftentimes, I get a phone call from a school principal to come train the young men in the school. When I arrive, I take a tour of the school, and I see 12-year old's, 13-year old's, and 14-year-old men!

How is this possible? How can you be a 40-year-old boy, but a 14-year-old man? Here's how:

Everything in that 14-year-old young man's life, he has taken full responsibility and accountability for. Cleaning his room, doing his homework, respecting the authority figure (parents & teachers). He does it no questions asked, and that makes him a man.

This male has earned the right to be called a man. I desire to be just like that 14-year-old man.

How about you?

1

CHOOSE TO BE A MAN

....

"Being a man has nothing to do with your age. You have to make a conscious decision to live a life of integrity."

....

GRADUATION DAY! JUNE 2003, THE DAY HAS FINALLY come. I am so happy to be done with school. Barely graduated with a C+ average, I earned just enough credits to slide across the stage and make my loved ones proud.

My inner circle, all the ones I deal with on a daily basis, is in attendance. My beautiful mother was elegantly dressed, with a smile that can light up a room. All of my siblings are excited for the big day and are eagerly waiting to take that famous cap and gown photo with me. My school mentors are lined up in formation patiently waiting to give that firm handshake to all that will be receiving this extraordinary honor.

And last, but not least, the man and the male are surprisingly both in attendance to take credit for the role they played during my academic journey. The man is calmly standing proud with a confidence that couldn't be shaken by a tsunami. The male is racing back and forth to show the audience that he is the one responsible for my accomplishment today.

Both individuals have made it a priority to attend this event but only one has chosen to be a man.

Which one is it? My Stepdad or my biological?

GRADUATION NIGHT OR GRADUATION YEAR?

Graduation night took on a life of its own with festivities that seemed to be never ending.

"What we drinking tonight, bro?" one of my classmates asked me with joy in his heart.

"I'm drinking whatever, man," was my response as I too was ready to indulge and show off my independence.

To my surprise, graduation night turned into many other nights of partying, drinking, and smoking. I can't believe how fast it all happened. I just graduated and it's already January. Where did six months go that fast? It's now back to the bitter cold months in Detroit and the weather is not the only thing that's being cold and heartless.

"Hello!" I angrily answer my pre-paid cell phone.

"Where the hell are you?" the response of my girlfriend that is eight months pregnant with my soon-to-be daughter.

"I'm watching tv. What do you want?" I said with an immature tone.

"You know what Baron? I ask you to come over here and help me today. I don't feel well, and I need to go to the doctor. I thought I could depend on you," she said as her voice cracked.

"What type of man are you? Do you even know how to be a man?" she yelled.

"I'm not in the mood for this today. I will call you back later," the phone slams with a loud click to end the call. Stressed out about being challenged by my girlfriend, I decided to contact my other female companion, who is more understanding and acceptable of my careless ways. I make the phone call and she arrived at my location with lighting speed.

"Hey baby," is my first statement as she rolls down the window.

"Hop in," is her reply as she welcomes me in her car to take me to my favorite McDonalds up the street.

A big mac, fries, cold sprite, and a pretty lady by my side is all I need at the moment. We eat and cruise the city without a care in the world. Me sitting on the passenger side being chauffeured around like a child. The only thing that is missing is me inside of a car seat like a newborn baby.

I should have gotten a "Happy Meal" to match the childlike behavior I am displaying. Now here it comes. The big question from her.

"When are you going to be my man? How long are we going to play this game?" she asked.

"Well you know, let's just see where things go. No need to rush into things. Besides, we are just having fun, right?" I replied with no intention of considering the questions that were just presented before me.

This was a common chess game that I often like to play because of my desire to have multiple women at my beck and call. Especially a woman with a car, her own place, a good job, and who is madly in love with me. This is the perfect catch! And if I play my cards right, she just may even help take care of my child that's on the way from a previous relationship. Life is good and at this point, I really don't have a care in the world.

How foolish was I?

"I will see you tomorrow, baby," I say to her as she drops me off in front of my mother's house. The feeling is almost like curbside service from your favorite Uber or Lyft driver.

"I love you, Baron. You are my everything. And I can't wait for you to be my man," was her response.

I wave goodbye to her as she sadly drives down the street, and then I turn around to face what would be the best accountability partner known to man. My sweet dear mother! I can see her face watching through the screen door and her eyes are saying everything – with no words being communicated. I walk slowly through the entrance and try to slide past her without entertaining the inevitable conversation.

Baron! she said with a tone only a mother could use when

she needs to get her child's attention. "What in the world is wrong with you? Why are you playing emotional games with multiple women? Why are you laying around here being lazy? Why are you wasting your potential? I did not raise you to behave like this!"

....

"When I was a child, I spoke as a child, I understood as a child, I behaved as a child. But when I became a MAN, I put away childish things."

-1 Cor. 13:11

....

WHEN WILL YOU CHOOSE TO BE A MAN?

Although my mother was a very loving person, she took no prisoners when it came to holding her children accountable, especially her young boys. My mother was not going to allow this foolishness to continue but for so long, and I knew my time was getting very thin with her.

"Baron, I'm going to make this very clear. You are either going to college or you're going to the military, but you ain't staying here! I raised you better than this. It's time for you to grow up and be a man!"

Like every other teenage boy who was not interested in hearing what his mother had to say, I went to my room and closed my door to have what would be a life-changing moment.

Because my feelings were now hurt from the harsh reality of where my life was headed, I was forced to do some reflecting. I was 19 years old, no job, child on the way, dating multiple women, drinking, smoking, having many close calls with the police, and most importantly, disappointing my sweet dear mother.

Although this had become a comfortable way for me to behave, the truth of the matter is that I was not raised like this. Like most teenage boys, I knew right from wrong. I had many examples in and outside of the home as to how to live my life as a man of integrity. All I had to do was CHOOSE!

I was a 19-year-old male on the verge of becoming a 20, 30, and 50-year-old male and it was seriously time for a change.

While lying on my bed feeling scared, hopeless, and unsure of what to do next, I saw a commercial on the TV: Accelerate your life today. Join the United States Navy!

I don't know if you have ever had the feeling of knowing when something is just right. It just feels good and you know you are making the right decision. Well, that's exactly how I felt when I saw that commercial. It just felt right. I saw how I would be able to leave my dangerous environment, make some money, see the world, and get a free education. This almost sounded too good to be true. I was sold immediately, plus I knew this would make my mother proud. I didn't entirely know if this was my life's calling, but I knew I had to choose to start being a responsible man and I needed some help as to how to do that! Just maybe the military would be the answer.

"Hello, my name is Baron Warren and I would like to join the Navy," was my greeting as I called the number that was in bold print on the TV screen.

"We will be right there." Click!

That's all that was said by the United States government, which left me very puzzled. I was hoping for some more details on the enlistment process, some cool navy stories, or at least a thank you for calling. Nope, I was received none of the above and now I was left with that strange feeling of uncertainty.

About 30 minutes passed and I heard a strange but firm knock on the door. As I opened the door with curiosity in my heart, I saw something that I had never seen before, at least not in person.

There stood two African American men in all white uniforms. They stood there with a boldness and confidence that seemed to be unshakeable. This may not be true, but it seemed like all the neighbors were outside and were staring at them. These men were clean, neat, well groomed, and clearly on a mission of some sort. And as strange as I felt, these men were actually there to see me.

"Hello, young man, are you Baron Warren"? The tallest one asked me with a commanding voice.

"Yeah, I'm Baron!" was my response in a shaky tone.

"Thank you, son, for calling us. We are so proud of you," the navy man said to me with a smile.

I replied, "why are you proud of me? What exactly did I do?"

He said, "today, Baron, you made the choice to be a man!"

ACTION STEPS

For every male reading the pages of this book, the message is very simple. In order to graduate from male-hood to manhood, you have to choose to be a man.

And let's be clear about something. You don't have to join the military to do that. All you have to do is identify and take full accountability on where your life is going, identify your opportunities and resources, decide to put away childish things, and make a conscious decision to live a life of integrity. That's it!

It's almost like graduating from high school, the only difference is the ceremony takes place every single day.

Here's the process. Every morning when you get out of the bed, you have to make the decision if you are going to be a male, or if you are going to be a man? Are you going to be a liar, or are you going to be honest? Are you going to be a thief, or are you going to add value to your community? Are you going to be lazy, or are you going to be responsible? Are you going to be a womanizer, or are you going to commit yourself to one woman? Are you going to have children and not be present, or are you going to make your children a priority and live for them!

Which is it going to be?

Here is the danger in this. This is not a onetime graduation. This is not a one-time ceremony. Any and every man can do the right thing for many, many years and choose to do the wrong thing with a snap of his finger. He can go out and be irresponsible, he can go back to being lazy and careless and he will go back to just being a male/boy. This can happen at any age.

But here is the good news and the main message for this book. No matter what has happened prior to you reading these pages. No matter what crime you have committed, person you have wronged, woman you have manipulated, children you have not made a priority, or time you have wasted, you have the power, right now, to choose to be a man.

This is good news!

If you are a teenage boy reading these pages, I challenge you to choose to be a man.

You just may be the only teenage man in the school. I promise you, this will bring much joy to your life, make your parents proud, and will take you to places beyond your wildest dreams.

If you are a young male reading these pages, maybe you are in your early twenties or thirties and unsure how to take the first major step in your life. This is it. Choose to be a man. I promise, this will be one of the best steps you will ever take in your life and will also equip you on how to make more positive and productive steps on your journey as a man.

If you are a male that happens to be incarcerated behind prison walls. Maybe you have made many poor decisions and feel like hope is lost. Maybe you think there is no way for you to turn your life around. My dear brother, choose to be a man today. I assure you if you take this step, you will never have to look over your shoulder again. You will never have to worry about living a life of crime, drugs, theft, or anything that has led you to these prison walls. If you choose to be a man, the spirit of integrity will be placed inside of you and you will be FREE indeed. Trust me.

To every male reading these pages, today and every day of the rest of your life is graduation day. I ask you to make the conscious decision to take the first step and choose to be a man!

2

DISCOVER THE CALLING FOR YOUR LIFE

"Every man has an assignment — some sort of calling.
It's your responsibility to discover what that is because you
weren't put on this earth to be mediocre.
Operate in your calling."

"SEAMAN WARREN! THE CHIEF OF THE SHIP IS CALLING you for a very important meeting," one of my shipmates yelled at me as I laid there in what would be my new home for many months to come, the USS Abraham Lincoln aircraft carrier, one of the Navy's finest ships. Home to approximately 5,000 hardworking Navy men!

I had now left the city of Detroit, completed the US Navy boot camp, and was at my first duty station in Seattle,

Washington. WOW! I had never thought I would leave the mean streets of Detroit. My mind could not see past my neighborhood. I thought everyone in the world lived exactly like me. I subconsciously thought that everyone lived in a state of poverty and hopelessness too.

But to my surprise, I had it all wrong, and I was now a Navy man, ready to see the world and experience new things. But what exactly? What was I called to do with my life?

As I ran up the many decks of the ship to get to my Chief's office, I was greeted by his strong, stern presence.

My Chief had a confidence about him that could challenge Mount Everest on any day of the week.

"Yes, Chief, you wanted to see me?" I respectfully stated to him.

"Yes, Seaman Warren, we have decided what you will do in the US Navy."

I was so excited. This was the moment I had been waiting for since I saw that cool navy commercial when I was back in Detroit, laying in my bed at my mother's house.

I saw the Navy men driving the ship through large bodies of waters with a smile that could light up the Pacific Ocean. I saw the skilled shooters protecting the country against enemy forces; I even saw the captain of the ship directing all of the sailors on the mission at hand. It was now my turn to experience the elite task as a Navy man!

"Seaman Warren, we are making you the ship's barber. Report to the barbershop immediately!"

"What!?" I responded with pain in my heart. "The ship's barber... Chief?" I asked again.

"Yes, Seaman Warren! Report there now!" he said in a non-negotiable manner.

Let me be clear about something for all you folks that may not be aware of military customs. Once you join the service and commit your life to protect and serve, your life is no longer yours. You are now government property, and with that being said, you are now told what to do.

In short, all the high-ranking superiors don't ask you anything, they tell you!

For anyone reading these pages that may be considering joining the military, understand that joining was one of the best decisions I have ever made in my life. It was also one of the toughest. So again, all that are considering joining the armed forces, please be aware of these details.

Now... moving on!

I was just told that I would be a barber for the duration of my military career, and I was crushed beyond words. This was not what I had signed up for. I did not see any barbers on the cool Navy commercials. What on earth did I get myself into? I wanted out immediately!

As I reported to the ship's barbershop, I was surprised that there were a few people that I knew from boot camp. In a way, this eased my heart a little, but I was still pretty upset. "A ship's barber?" I would often repeat to myself in my mind. "I know I wasn't called to do this with my life!" SMH!

I was forced to become something I had never even considered being, and it felt like all was lost. But as I write these words and look back on this experience, I can say with full confidence that this would be the beginning of me discovering my calling. The barber's life on board a US Navy ship consisted of the following:

I had to first learn how to give a standard military-style haircut, and then I had to get comfortable with cutting at least 20 sailors' hair per day, seven days a week. There are no weekends when out to sea in the Navy!

The last and maybe the most important thing I had to learn was the art of communication. Now some would ask, why is it so important to be a great communicator as a barber? I'm glad you asked.

Being a good barber in any capacity requires excellent grooming skills as well as good professionalism and or conversation. I had no idea that the art of communication would be a huge benefit for me. I had been a great communicator my entire life — just needed a little direction to tap into my God-given talent/calling!

As I began my career as the ship's barber, something strange began to happen during my long days out to sea. Not only did I become very comfortable with making all the sailors look good with a quality haircut, but I began to develop another skill that I didn't know would provide a ton of value to people in need. That skill was listening!

I began to notice that sailors were not just coming to me for a quality haircut, but they were coming to me to share what was on their hearts. They were coming to get away from the long days on the ship and have a place to relax. They were coming to me to share their problems. In short, they were coming to me because they felt comfortable to share their feelings with a trustworthy listening ear.

After about a full year of serving onboard the ship in the barbershop, my eyes began to open. I realized I was not just grooming these men's outer appearance; I was also grooming their minds. Cutting hair and communicating with the men now became grooming for the soul. They felt so validated and appreciated after spending 20 minutes in my barber chair. Many of them would say, "Hey, Warren. I really don't need a haircut, but can I stop by for a while just to have a chat?"

I began to find purpose beyond the barber chair. I began to see much more potential in myself and the different and unique ways I could add value to the lives of men I served. My mind began to explore different ways to problem solve, and I would share it with those who may have been facing serious life circumstances. Soon, I became more interested in what made men successful and what steps they should take to have the healthy relationships and the best quality of life. Listening, communicating, and counseling these men in need gave me so much joy. I had now discovered my life's calling!

Growing up, I never once said that I wanted to be a barber or a counselor. How in the world did I stumble upon, what was now crystal clear to me, definitely my life's calling. What I came to understand that being a barber wasn't necessarily the calling, counseling men in need was. But this discovery would have never happened if I wasn't forced into an uncomfortable situation that would ultimately lead me down this extraordinary path. In some strange way, I was able to learn how to tap into my gift as a counselor while working as a barber aboard a military ship in the middle of the Pacific Ocean during a time of war, following 9/11.

This was definitely not the plan I had in mind for my life, but because I opened my heart in an uncomfortable situation, this gave me the power to operate my gift to the world and discover my life's calling.

··

"Therefore, my brothers and sisters, make every effort to confirm your calling and election. For if you do these things, you will never stumble."
-2 Peter 1:10

··

ACTION STEPS

Just for a moment, I want you to reflect on your life and think about the things that brought you the most joy. I want you to identify a time where you were able to add value to someone's life. This may not necessarily be at a place of employment, or this may be a time where you weren't paid for it. I just want you to reflect on the moments of your life where you felt complete joy doing something you love to do. Maybe to the point that you would even do it free of charge. Whatever that is, there is a strong possibility that it is what you have been called to do.

The old saying goes that "if you find something you love to do, you will never work a day in your life!" I believe this old saying has a lot of truth behind it, and it has become one of my life philosophies. But let me add a little something to it.

There is a secret that all males must understand during their journey to manhood. Here it is!

The moment you discover what your purpose is for your life, the moment you discover your mission, your assignment, your calling, you are no longer an ordinary man. You are now Superman!

Something magical happens when you operate your God-given gift. You gain a sense of purpose, accomplishment, motivation, and self-worth.

When it's time to get up in the morning, you will no longer moan, drag, and complain when preparing for the day. You will no longer roll out of bed. You will now bounce out of bed.

There's a big difference between the two!

Your calling becomes a part of who you are, and you will find yourself always ready to serve any, and everywhere you go. This is a feeling that goes beyond the fulfillment of having a job.

When you discover what you have been called to do, you will no longer report to work. Every day, for the rest of your life, you will now report to your calling!

The even better news about discovering your calling is that your gift to the world adds value to someone's life. That gift, skill, or service that you love to provide can possibly turn into money to provide for you and your family!

As a man, it is critical to be in a position to make yourself marketable to be gainfully employed. That being said, it has become clear to me that money is connected to value, and if you line all these things up (your gift to the world, value to someone like an employer) you have now hit the sweet spot to have an excellent quality of life as a man!

GIVE YOUR ABILITY A RESPONSIBILITY

To the teenage male that may be thinking it is too early to think about the calling for your life. Let me be clear, it is never too early to discover your life's mission.

I believe that the sooner any male discovers his calling, the better. Many men have wasted years of going from job to job in search of what will give them the fulfillment of self-worth. For many, it has been a big waste of time. So, if you are a teenager or young adult, now is the perfect time to take charge of your life and seek out what brings you the most joy. I want to personally encourage you not to waste another minute, discover your calling today. Your time is one of your most valuable assets. As a young man, you are in a very good position. Use it wisely!

For the seasoned and senior males who may be reading these pages. Because you have had years of life experience, that doesn't mean it's too late for you. Your gift to the world never changes just because you only have a few more years on this earth. Your gift is still valuable, and you can still operate your gift in any area of your life.

That being said, if you are a plumber, identify how you can use your gift for the world, combine it with plumbing, and take care of your family like your life depends on it. If you are a janitor, identify the things you know you enjoy doing, combine it with being a janitor, operate in your calling, and take care of your family with a smile, like your life depends on it.

The point I'm making is, it doesn't matter where you are in your life. You have the power to discover your calling in this season. Today! It took me to be forced to be a barber to discover my calling. It is my belief that God showed me my calling through cutting hair because I opened my heart to serve others.

To the older men that may be in an uncomfortable season of your life, I challenge you to identify your gifts and talents, put it towards your current job, and allow God to show you your life calling. You have the power to do this, men!

YOU MADE A MISTAKE, BUT YOU'RE NOT A MISTAKE

For the man who may be incarcerated and feeling like all is lost -- that there can't possibly be a way for you to discover your calling -- maybe you made poor decisions in the past and feel like you don't have much to offer society. I would like to say this in the most dramatic way possible: YOU MADE A MISTAKE, BUT YOU ARE NOT A MISTAKE!

Every single man walking the earth right now, worldwide, in prison or out of prison still has an assignment for his life. Sometimes our assignments change depending on the season of our life that we are currently in. For men that are incarcerated, this is a unique season. That doesn't mean you can't operate in your gift. Your gift to the world is still valuable, even in prison!

So, to the men who may have a two-year sentence, to the men who will be serving the rest of their days on earth behind prison walls, let me encourage you in the most respectful way to take the challenge, discover your calling, and be of service to any and every one in need of your gift. Your gifts and talents were not designed for you to keep and take to the graveyard. Your gift was designed for you to give back to society.

The world needs your gift! Once you discover it, I'm confident that this will give you a sense of joy and peace that will soar over prison walls and beyond.

I guarantee it!

3

BE A LIFELONG LEARNER

....

"In order for a man to lead his home and be able to provide value to his community, and value to his wife and children, he has to always be learning."

....

"I<small>T NEVER RAINS IN</small> S<small>OUTHERN</small> C<small>ALIFORNIA</small>!" I <small>SCREAMED</small> out the window of my truck as I was cruising down the 1 highway on the most beautiful coast known to man. The California Coast is absolutely breathtaking!

For those of you that have never had the opportunity to enjoy the coast of Los Angeles, please try to get there. It is such a treat to watch the waves splash up against the sands of California beaches. You can't help but be in awe as you stare at the homes of some of the wealthiest people in the country. It is still one of my favorite places to experience, and I had the pleasure of finishing my time in the Navy in this beautiful area.

I was down to my last two years of service, and I knew my time was getting very short. Every day, I would think about what would be the next chapter of my life? I had chosen to be a man by putting away childish things and living a life of integrity. I had discovered my gift/calling as a counselor and was operating in that calling on a daily basis, both at work and within my family. But now came the time for me to challenge my thinking.

It was now time for me to enhance the gifts that God had given me. But how would I do that? Where would I start? I must admit, I was a little nervous.

"Daddy, Daddy," my beautiful daughter would oftentimes yell to me. "Where are we going today?" she would ask with optimism in her heart.

"We are going to drive all around the world," I would say just to get that look of excitement out of her.

These were some magical times when I would put both of my daughters in the car, and the three of us would just explore the world. It was always a new experience, no matter where we went. As I grew as a man and a father, it began to dawn on me that my daughters were expecting me to always have an answer for them regarding our travel plans.

It didn't matter what we were doing or where we were going, my daughters would ask for details, and I had better say something that made sense in their little minds. This became quite the task because I knew I could not let my little ladies down. They were counting on me to explain the mission for the day. So, with that, I knew that if I didn't know the details, I better learn it quickly or I would be held accountable. I believe that this was when learning became a priority in my life.

"Petty Officer Warren, get in my office right now!" my new supervisor yelled as he requested my presence in his office for what sounded like a serious emergency.

"Yes, Chief Robinson," I promptly answered.

"I see you have about two years left on your obligation with the military. What are your plans for the future, sailor?"

I replied, "well, Chief, I was thinking about going to college!" This was definitely not my real desire, but it sounded like the right thing to say at the time.

"Well, what are you waiting for? Go get registered for classes right now and report back to me immediately!" he replied.

OMG! I had now put myself in a situation that would force me to follow through on a task that I had no intention of accomplishing. I had just arrived in sunny California, and I had no desire to spend any of my time in a classroom. I was making good money, had a nice car, a nice townhouse, and my kids were well taken care of. Life was great! Why mess up a good thing, I thought? But as I reflect on that time in my life, Chief Robinson knew something that I didn't. He had wisdom beyond my years and was actually challenging me to maximize my potential and put myself in a better position to be of value to my family and community long term. I'm so happy he did.

The beauty of being in the military is that a college education is 100% free. All you have to do is show and pass the class. That's it. But you wouldn't believe that only about 20-30% of service members actually go to school. This is a huge opportunity that so many service members regret later in life.

As I arrived at the Navy College office, I was greeted by a very friendly academic counselor. "How can I help you today?" she asked with a big smile!

"I'm here to enroll in college, but I'm not sure where to begin," I replied with a smug look.

"Ok, tell me what do you want to study? Tell me what you are passionate about," she said!

For some reason, at that moment, something excited me when I was asked that question. I began to reflect on how I had made the transition from male to MAN and was now operating in my calling as an honorary counselor. I reflected on all the people I helped on board my ship, how I loved to speak at corporate events, and how I loved to volunteer around my local community. I didn't know exactly what I wanted to study, but I knew I wanted to be of service to those in need. I wanted to continue to help people in a more professional way. I wanted to learn about what causes some of the people's daily problems, and I wanted to learn a way to help them.

I did my very best to share my heart with my academic counselor. To my surprise, she sat there the entire time with a unique grin on her face. It was as if she knew something magical was about to happen.

In the gentlest way, she said, "Petty Officer Warren, I think you should pursue a degree in psychology!"

"PSYCHOLOGY?" I replied in a strange way.

Let me be clear, for all that are reading these pages, being a poor boy from the ghetto streets of Detroit, I don't think I ever even said the word "psychology." So, my comprehension could not process what it was, nor was I interested in studying it.

"Just take one course, and if you don't like it, we can always try something else," she stated.

"Ok... If you think its best. I guess I can give it a shot." What in the world was I doing! I reported back to my Chief and proudly said, "I enrolled in college, Chief! I will be studying Psychology!

I kid you not, he looked at me and gave me the exact same unique smile that the academic counselor gave me. It was like they both knew something I didn't and were working on a devious plan for me. All I know is that my Chief and academic counselor were both interested in the journey I was about to embark on.

WOW!

About a few weeks had passed, and it was now time for me to attend class. I think it may be fair to say that I was not a happy camper. All the thoughts in my mind were negative, and I had a feeling of "I can't do this. I'm just not smart enough to be in college!" It was as if I had already given up before the instructor even stepped into the classroom. I was ready to throw in the towel.

It is my personal belief that God always presents interesting ways to get your attention when you are feeling doubtful. I don't know if it was part of his plan, but when my instructor came into the room, he did not look like what I expected at all. In all honesty, I'm not sure what I expected, but I just know I was not expecting a short, Latin, middle-aged man. For some reason, he looked pretty cool to me, and I became very interested in what he had to say.

From the first day of class, this man blew me away with the power of words and his gentle, yet informative knowledge of psychology and the power of the human mind! Each class became an out-of-body experience, and it felt like I began to discover brains I never knew I had. At times, it felt like the instructor was taking us on a field trip and showing us if we commit to learning, the sky is the limit to how far we could go in our life.

For two years straight, education became a priority, and then I officially became a lifelong learner.

Now let's be clear. College was not all sunshine and rainbows. I had to put in some long hours while sacrificing time away from my family to accomplish the goal of obtaining my college degree. But as God as my witness, this was so well worth it. Going to college was much more beyond just obtaining a piece of paper. College introduced me to a new way of thinking. My appetite for reading became stronger. My abilities as a father became more enhanced. My financial management became more organized. And the list goes on and on.

Here's the point. A college degree may not be for every male making his transition to MANHOOD, but it was the platform that allowed me to tap into this critical step. College gave me the desire to become a lifelong learner.

What's your platform?

ACTION STEPS

When I was growing up during my childhood years, I absolutely hated school. I didn't do well at all. I barely graduated from high school, and I believe it only happened because of God's grace and mercy. But please hear my heart on this. Once I grew up and became a MAN, once I started having children, once I started applying for jobs, once I got married and started to lead my family, a profound awakening came over me. And here it is: how am I going to be successful in any of these things if I don't know anything?!"

- If all I know is my favorite rap song, how am I going to lead a family to greatness?
- If all I know is my favorite football team, how am I going to get a good job?
- If all I care about is chasing multiple women, how am I going to set a good example for my kids?

The message in this chapter is that your becoming a lifelong learner is mandatory. You have to do this! Nobody on this earth can learn for you. You have to learn for you.

For the young man who is going through school right now and may think it's a waste of time. Trust me; it's not. Cherish this time during your adolescent years and position yourself to be ready for the next chapter of your life (college, military, trade school). Doing your best right now will definitely make life much easier for you in the long run. I guarantee it!

For the young adult who may still be trying to find your way. No matter what job you are working right now, take time to invest in your education so you can lead you and your family to greatness.

Your wife, children, and siblings are looking to you to lead the family. That's what being a man is all about. So that being said, you have to stay filled up with knowledge so you can pass it on to those who are watching you. So cut the TV off sometimes and invest in your learning. Your family depends on you!

For the men who may be incarcerated. Step away from the weight pit! Yes, I said it, and I stand by this statement. Oftentimes, I see men in prison, making lifting weights their top priority. Men, being the strongest guy in the room, is not going to help you lead a family to greatness. It's not going to help you become gainfully employed nor help you make the smooth transition back into society.

I'm not bashing lifting weights, but it can't be your life's priority. Use this time to better yourself. Don't let 5, 10, 20 years go by, and all you have to show for it is your ability to lift weights. Go home a changed man by investing in your education.

Men. Deciding to become a lifelong learner is not a one-time thing. It's forever. You have to always be learning. You have to graduate to the next level every day. Once you become a lifelong learner, you will forever be valuable to your wife, children, and community.

Forever!

4

DELIGHT YOURSELF IN RESPONSIBILITY

"This is so important for young, black men. Whether it's taking care of your children or paying bills, be delighted to take care of your business without having an attitude."

SOMETIMES LIFE JUST THROWS YOU A CURVEBALL!

I was back in Detroit, where it all began. I had an extraordinary experience serving my country in the US Navy for eight consecutive years. I had traveled the world, lived across the country, made good money, and all the while, I never thought I would ever come back to the place of my humble beginnings. I had completed a degree in psychology and was now honorably discharged with nothing but hope and optimism in my heart. I believe it's fair to say that a lot of service members believe that when you leave the military, there will be just a world of jobs waiting on you when you return to your hometown. I had no idea that I to would be faced with the harsh realities of transitioning back from a military man -- to a civilian.

With no job, not much money saved, recently divorced, and the father of two kids, I literally had to move back into my mother's house. I believe this may have been one of the most humbling experiences of my entire life, and I was not thrilled about it at all.

For the first 30 days after my arrival back in Detroit and the start of my new civilian life, I didn't do much of anything. I would wake up and aimlessly let the day float by. My motivation was kind of dead, and it may be fair to say that I had a bit of an attitude. I was upset that my marriage had ended. I was upset that the government didn't have a job waiting on me when I arrived back in Michigan after serving the US honorably. I was bitter at the fact that I was back in my parents' home and had to play by the rules. To me, it was all bad, and in a way, I felt like a failure.

Around the second month of my so-called depression and feeling sorry for myself, my daughters came to spend the weekend with me. This was such an unusual circumstance because they had always had their own room in our own house. But now they were with dad, in the backroom of Grandma's house, and they were kind of clueless as to what caused the change.

As we sat there watching tv and trying to enjoy what would now be our private time in my childlike bedroom, my youngest daughter made a powerful statement that I will never forget. She said...

"Daddy, when are you getting your own house?"

As my eyes popped wide open and I cut the light on in dramatic fashion, I couldn't believe that she had asked me this question, and in the concerned tone she delivered it in. With emotion in my heart, I said,

"What did you say, baby girl"?

She then not only repeated the statement, but she added a few choice words. She said, "Daddy, what's going on? You need your own house. My sister and I want our own room again!"

After noticing the seriousness in her eyes, I began to tell her my very long sob story. I mean, I explained it all! I spoke on how the government did me wrong, the effects of a divorce, why I didn't have a job at the moment, how things were expensive, how the White man is always mistreating the Black man. I even spoke on how my biological father wasn't in my life and how that played a part in me being irresponsible and not being a good steward with my time and money. I mean, you name it, I gave every excuse known to man.

In the great words of the man who raised me, my father, Louis Holley, "I had more excuses than a guy going to jail!"

Now, this is where the story gets interesting. After I finished what would be an award-winning performance as to why my two beautiful daughters and I were now living in my mother's back room, my youngest yet again asked me something that has forever changed my life. She simply said, "so dad, what are you going to do about it?"

It would be extremely hard for me to explain the emotions I felt after hearing that statement from my precious daughter. Up until that point, I was having what some would call a serious pity party.

In just a little over 30 days, I had gotten really comfortable with shifting the blame as to why I was in the circumstance I was in, why I was unemployed, why I didn't have much money, why I was now divorced, and why my kids didn't have a place they could call home. I had gotten a little comfortable being irresponsible! But because of God's grace and mercy, he sent a messenger to remind me to get up, wipe them tears, and start being responsible again. And that messenger he sent was my daughter, Jordane Warren.

....

Responsibility:
*The opportunity or ability to act independently
and make decisions with pride.*

....

Now, I don't think I did much that very night, but that very next morning, I was like a lion on the prowl. The voice of my daughter just kept ringing through my head. Not only was she right, but I didn't want her to think that her daddy was a bum. I couldn't live with the fact of knowing that she may think her dad was lazy or irresponsible. I had to do something and fast.

I got up that next morning and inquired about every available job known to man in the city of Detroit. I mean, I called everywhere. I didn't care if it was full time, part-time, short time, or some time, I was ready to work and bring that quality of life back to my girls and me. For the next 90 days, I didn't get anything, and I must admit that I was feeling a little discouraged yet again. "How could this be? How on earth could I be stuck in this situation?" I thought.

As I reflect on the past, the only thing I can say is that in life, sometimes it's just going to be hard as a man. It doesn't always make sense, and it's not always fair, but as a man with serious responsibilities now (wife, children, home, finances), it can just be a little overwhelming.

But here is the good news. Men are equipped to handle life's problems, so it is never impossible to rise above life challenges. There is always a resource or some type of lifeline to be productive and provide for your family. My lifeline was on the way and actually came through a personal military friend.

Just around that 90th day of job searching, my good friend

G. Lawson called me. We had actually met in the Navy and served on the same ship together out in Seattle, Washington. Coincidentally, we were both home and back in Detroit on the same mission. A JOB! He called me and said, "Hey, Warren, come with me to this veterans job fair, bro! I hear there will be a ton of employers there, and we may be able to find some employment!" Without any hesitation, I jumped at the opportunity and met him there!It was almost like this event was truly ordained by God because the first employer I met hired me right there on the spot. I was so excited that I believe I asked to work that same day.

Now let me be clear, this particular job was not my dream job at all, but it provided something that was far more important to me at the moment. I wanted my kids to know that dad was responsible and was very much delighted to take care of them.

Within six months of working that new job, I had saved up a good amount of money, put a down payment on a new apartment in the suburbs, maintained a good running car, and most importantly, my girls had their rooms back. This really made me feel good. This really made me feel like a man. I was delighted to be a productive citizen again. I was delighted to be providing for my children. I was delighted to be responsible!

ACTION STEPS

Men, I'm sure at some point in your life you have been told to be responsible. It may have started with your parents or guardian, at school, from your employer, or maybe your spouse or another family member. The point is, we have all heard this statement before. But I intentionally changed up this idea and added the word *delighted* to the quote.

Here's why!

It's one thing to do something and moan and complain while doing it. It's a totally different experience when you take joy in the task of the day, no matter how challenging it may be. The circumstances change when you focus on the importance of why you're doing that task. So in short, whatever is going on in your life, whatever bills you have to pay, job you have to report to, children that you gave life to and that you now have to provide for, community you have to impact in a positive way, influence you will have on someone, whatever business you are responsible for, take care of it, just do it, and *do it without having an attitude*!

Every male making the transition from male-hood to manhood has some type of responsibility in his life. The only way to achieve it in the most impactful way is to not only be responsible but be delighted to be responsible. Everyone that sees you taking care of your business must know you are proud to do so! Here are a few quick pointers:

For the young man living with his parents, when it's time to clean your room, take out the trash, do your homework, being obedient to the authority figure (your parents), don't just be responsible, be delighted to be responsible. Do all of your tasks without being told. This will build a level of trust between you and your parents that will forever be cherished.

For the adult man, when you are looking for that job, or when you are taking care of your wife and children, paying your bills on time, being a pillar to your society, do everything with a delightful tone. This does not necessarily mean having a permanent smile on your face all day, every day. What I am saying is that your wife, children, and community should never feel like you are a burden to them. They should never feel like you are getting on their nerves and you hate adding value to their life, NO! They should always feel like you're delighted to go to work, pay the bills, protect the family, and influence the community. You are delighted to be responsible.

To the man doing time behind prison walls. Here is something that I want you to hear from my heart to yours, and I mean this in the most respectfully way. You become a man when you take full responsibility for your actions. When you sincerely take ownership of your actions and apologize for your mistakes, that becomes a monumental moment in your life. That being said, take full ownership for any mistakes you have made and be delighted to make it right.

That may mean serving your time in a respectable way. That may mean adding value to your peers who you see every day on the yard. The point is that, even behind prison walls, you have the power to be delighted to be responsible. So, with these words of love, my brother, whatever business you have to take care of while you serve your time (good behavior, employment readiness, GED, time served), be sure to delight yourself in responsibility!

In closing this chapter, I would like to ask all the MEN reading these pages for a special favor. This favor may sound strange, but this will be of great value to you and your family.

Here it is:

Please take the word *contribute*
out of your vocabulary.

This word, or should I say, this mindset, has gotten a lot of men in trouble for many years. This word is a recipe for disaster and should be removed from every man's vocabulary.

There is a big difference between "contribute" and provide." I don't *contribute to* my kids' wellbeing; I *provide for* their wellbeing. When they say, "Dad, do you have money for food?" I never respond back by saying, "Well, I think I can contribute!"

Sounds strange, doesn't it?

Your wife and children don't need you to go 50/50 with them. They need you to provide for them. They need you to have the mindset of a provider.

And with that mindset, you will forever be delighted to be responsible!

5
HELP ANOTHER MALE BECOME A MAN

"As one of my favorite authors, the late Dr. Myles Munroe, said, 'Success without a successor is failure.' Men have to go get men. Go out there and be important to your society."

"SOMETHING IS MISSING IN MY LIFE!" I SAID TO MYSELF AS I walked the prison yard at one of the largest correctional facilities in the state of Michigan. Not only did I accept the offer of a better, high-paying job as a correctional officer, but my life seemed to be back to the quality of life I once had when I was in the military.

It's customary for veterans to discharge from the military and become civil servants and wear the uniform to protect and serve again. The most common jobs for veterans are police officers, firefighters, paramedics, and yes, prison guards.

I had made the transition from active duty military man to a civilian correctional officer, and I was essentially back to what was the norm for me. Protecting and serving my community. I was back to making the good, stable money that I had grown so accustomed to from my time in the military. I had my nice car and condo again, and last but not least, my daughters were looking at me with that special twinkle in their eye. This look from them was worth a million bucks in my world!

But with all this going on, I still felt a sense of emptiness inside. I felt like I needed to be doing something else, but what exactly?

I would face yet another life-changing moment that would shift me in the direction of personal growth as a man, and my final step on this journey to manhood! It happened on a hot summer day when all the men inside of the prison were out doing their regular workout sessions. Lifting weights in the prison weight pit is a top priority for most men serving time. In every prison in America, the weight pit can be an interesting place, but if not careful, it can also be a dangerous one as well.

As a new officer, I found myself having many conversations with the residents during my shift. I would also find myself in many debates with them that would leave me tired, frustrated, and upset most of the time. It's funny because when I think back on this time in my life, I recall all of the more seasoned officers never having these types of problems that us rookies would have.

They knew the art of doing their jobs without letting the job or the people get the best of them. But of course, like most rookies, I was on a mission to prove I was equipped for the job, and I would entertain any and every conversation known to man.

This one particular day, I got into a huge debate over good, bad, what's right, what's wrong, and a number of other crazy subject matters that did nothing but send me on a crazy and pointless whirlwind amongst the population.

Near the end of this loud and heated debate with this man that had served nearly a combined 20 years in prison, he said something that shocked me beyond words. Our conversation had led me to make the statement of "these are the prison rules, you are in prison, and you must follow them, sir!" With boldness in his tone and anger in his eyes, he replied very loudly,

"I'm not in prison; you're in prison,
Officer Warren. I'm at home!"

I kid you not, when he said this statement, it literally scared the daylights out of me. In my short time as a correctional officer, I had never heard anyone make such a bold statement like this.

Let me explain more!

What this individual was saying to me is that he believes and accepts that this caged, barbed-wire-fenced, and heavily controlled institution was no longer just a place for him to visit and pay his debt to society, but it was now his home for the rest of his days here on earth.

I think it's also important that I mention that this man was not serving a life sentence. He had actually been in and out of prison his entire adult life and was up for parole yet again. He didn't have to make prison his home, but he CHOSE to do so!

The point I'm making is that this man was making it clear to me that I was a visitor, but in his mind, he was content with making the prison system his home. He was saying that there is nothing out in the free world for him, and he will make no more efforts to live a life outside of prison walls.

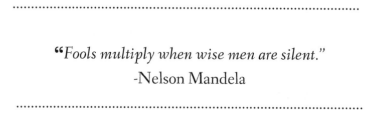

"*Fools multiply when wise men are silent.*"
-Nelson Mandela

Believe it or not, this is the mindset of so many men, not just in prison, but worldwide today. Some have gotten to a place of hopelessness and despair and see no other way to live their life but in destructive conditions. (gangs, drugs, violence, womanizing, laziness, prison)

This statement forever changed me and gives me chills right now as I write these words.

About two weeks later, my supervisor asked me to conduct some training with a few men inside the prison. It had become known around the prison that I was a great communicator, and I was always asked to train and speak at ceremonies and training events. So, without hesitation, I jumped at the opportunity to train some of the men.

To my surprise, when I entered the training room, I saw that same man I had the heated discussion with just two weeks prior. We were both fully aware of our feelings towards one another, but something in the air was a little different from our first meeting. It's hard for me to say, but I just knew this encounter would be different from the first, and I told myself that I would not mess up this golden opportunity.

For about one hour straight, I spoke to him and about 30 other men on the importance of them being honest men. I gave them tools on how they can remove fear from their lives if they decide to live a life of integrity!

As I was ended my talk, I looked over in the corner, and I saw something that I was not prepared to see. That same man who I had the headed conversation with just two weeks prior to this training was now literally crying real tears in the corner of the room and was full of emotion.

Keep in mind, we are in a prison, and seeing a man cry is not the usual. Some would argue that crying in prison can actually be dangerous and send the message to other prisoners that you are weak or a pushover.

But I tell you, this man was not a weak individual. He was a very bold and strong man with lots of respect amongst the prison population. But this particular day, none of that mattered. Something I said that day resonated with him. It was as if he had some type of epiphany, and he was ready for change. After noticing this shocking situation, I immediately cleared out the room of all the other prisoners, just leaving him and me there alone. I walked over to him, and politely said, "Are you ok, Sir?" He lifted up his head and responded by saying this:

> "Officer Warren, my entire life, I thought I knew what it meant to be a man, but obviously I don't. I thought gang banging, drugs, having a lot of women, and coming to prison made me a man, but that's a lie. I don't know where to begin. I don't know what it really means to be a true man of integrity."

At that very moment, my life became complete. I knew what was missing in my life. I immediately became aware of the last step that every man must achieve on the journey to manhood! With love in my heart, I looked at him and said, "Sir, someone had to help me become a man, and it would be my pleasure to help you!"

He jumped up, we embraced each other as men, and I knew right then and there that this was something I had to commit to for the rest of my days. I had to commit my life to *helping males become men.*

Several months after this life-changing event, I would work my way up the corporate ladder to Prison Counselor while serving at multiple facilities throughout the state of Michigan. My passion for helping males become men began to grow beyond my initial intentions within the prison system. I began to travel and speak at prisons outside of Michigan, and my appetite to operate in this manner began to grow even more. The final moment to seal my fate is when I came home and saw my eldest daughter, Alecia Warren standing in the kitchen. She noticed something was heavy on my heart, and she asked me what was wrong.

I told her that I believe that God had been leading me to quit my job and serve the men in this capacity full time. I also explained to her how scared I was and had never considered being self-employed. "I must be crazy!!!" I said to her. "How on earth could I even think of doing something like this!"

With full confidence, as if she was as wise as a 60-year-old woman, she gently said, "do it, daddy. This is what you have been called to do. We will be fine. The men need your help!"

Yet again, I was embraced by the love and support of my children, who gave me the power to complete this final task on my journey to manhood. You wouldn't believe this to be true, but that very next day, I quit my job, started my own speaking and coaching business and have been serving the men in the area of personal growth ever since!

There have been many ups and downs, but overall this has been a fantastic experience, and it truly feels good to be operating in my true calling as a speaker while helping males in need. As of today, I have spoken and trained nationwide and abroad, and the "*5 Steps to Manhood*" journey has been nothing less than extraordinary.

It is with love and complete sincerity that these steps I have shared with you have touched your heart. It's my hope that this final step and the closing of this curriculum equips you for greatness! Men, always remember to stay humble on your journey, identify where you are needed, and help a MALE become a MAN!

ACTION STEPS

When I saw the commercial to join the United States Military, I was very impressed and called the number right away. Those men showed up to my doorsteps within 20 minutes, and you could tell that they meant business. When I opened the door, they said something to me that forever changed my life.

Here's what they said:

"Baron, why are you sagging your paints, Sir"?

"Baron, why is their loud music with profanity being played around woman and children, Sir?"

"Baron, why haven't you shaved your face today, Sir?"

And the most memorable question of them all was...

"Baron, what's that smell? Why does your house smell suspect?" as the aroma of marijuana was dangerously obvious.

These men didn't even say hello to me. When I opened the door, they immediately began asking tough questions that no one had asked me in a long time. Although I was raised in an awesome Christian home, at this stage in my life, no one was holding me accountable as a man. It was accountability time, and these were the men for the job. Then, after what seemed like a long list of questions, they said something that forever touched my soul. They said, "Baron, it's clear you don't know what it means to be a man. But we are going to help you, sir!"

What every man must understand is that you can't be a real man and complete your task as a man unless you train another male to take your place. Every man should be identifying the males in his area, neighborhood, church, job, school, and mentor them. The good news is that every single man is in a position to do this. Here's how:

For the young man in grade school, be a leader and not a follower. Set the example for your peers and show them how a MAN should behave at school. Take your little brother by the hand and show him the things you have already learned in your young years. Every little brother

49

automatically looks up to his big brother, so this is an easy job. At school, the younger males always want to be just like the older males, so this also an easy job for mentorship. Find a male that needs some assistance and respectfully show him the way to MANHOOD! 10, 12, 15, or 18 years of age, it doesn't matter. You can be a mentor to a male in need!

For the adult man who is young, smart, strong, and full of life and wisdom. Find a male at your job, at your college, church, or neighborhood and mentor them. Show them that being well-groomed is mandatory for every man. Encourage them to pursue education so they can become more marketable to take care of a family. Show them that rap, tv, sports, and partying should not be a priority in a man's life, but being the pastor, protector, and provider of the home is. There are many adult males that can use your wisdom. Go find them and help those males become MEN of integrity!

For my brothers behind prison walls. My dear brothers! You are in an extraordinary position to change the world. You have an opportunity that a lot of men don't have. You know exactly what happens when you make a few poor decisions, and your freedom is taken away. I can only imagine how painful this is, but you do have the power to use it for good.

When that new crazy kid gets off the bus, enters the prison, and thinks he knows it all and he has life figured out. When he walks around the prison yard as if he has a badge of honor for coming to prison. When he disrespects the staff and the rules of the institution, when it's obvious he needs some direction on how to be a man, *help him!*

You have the power to mentor him. Tell him about your experiences in prison. Tell him how you wish you could do things differently. Tell him how you haven't seen your mother, wife, and children in many years. Tell him how drugs have robbed you of precious time with your family. Whatever your story is that landed you in prison, tell a male in need and help him grow to be a man of integrity. There are young males and old males right now on the prison yard that needs to hear your story. You have the power to change their lives.

Go find him and mentor him!

A MOTHER'S LOVE

"A child's first teacher is its mother."

-Peng Liyuan

As I write these words, my heart literally aches and fills with emotion. My mind wanders to a place of love and fear all at the same time. As I write these words, I can't help but wonder, where are the fathers? As I write these words, there are millions of mothers worldwide doing the difficult task of raising their boys alone, by themselves, and not with much support from the male who has not made his role as a father a priority.

As I write these words, all I can say is, *I'm sorry* to all the mothers that are forced to turn males into men alone. In the same breath, I am in awe of a love that is unbelievable in every way. This type of love has the power to make a dollar stretch to feed an entire family, the power to recognize the cry of her child while in the midst of many other children, the strength to endure the pains of watching her son be incarcerated and still support him day after day, the power to help with homework, wash the clothes, cook the food, attend her son's basketball game, work a job or several, and still manage to maintain through the trials and tribulations of life.

I write these words with nothing but admiration in my heart and joy in my soul to witness such love.

I write these words because of my years of traveling the world, speaking nationwide and abroad, coaching thousands of people, I have never seen anything more powerful than *A Mother's Love!*

I write these words with the utmost respect and pure intentions. It is my prayer that my suggestions be considered not as a demand, but as a guideline and a blessing when raising your young son into a man. I humbly make these suggestions with love!

Let's begin! There are only two steps that I will make in this book when raising your male into the MAN that God has called him to be. It is my belief that if applied correctly, this will be life-changing for your son and put him on track to maximize his potential.

STEP #1: HOLD HIM ACCOUNTABLE!

Mothers, the best thing you can do for your son, to ensure that he will be respectful, responsible, independent, hardworking with good integrity, treat women right, be honest, and a MAN of God, is to hold him accountable.

Let me explain what I mean by this. The few traits I listed above – regarding what you want your son to become – must be instilled in him. Not only should these points be driven into the core of his soul, but they should also have firm consequences when they are not displayed. What I'm trying to say is that the earlier he knows what these things are, and the sooner he understands that you will hold him accountable to these things with firm consequences, the better he will be.

This rule actually should not just be applied to your son, but for any male for that matter. Let me be clear, a young male, an old male, your son, your brother, your boyfriend, your husband is only going to go as far as you let him. Therefore, for any male in your life, including your son, the best thing you can do for him is to hold him accountable for his actions as a man.

Your son needs to understand the power of the word *consequence*. Now, most of us use that word in a negative way. But the truth is, a consequence is simply the results of your actions. So, if your son does all of his schoolwork and completes all of the required credits through his academic years, the consequence will be him graduating with a diploma. But if he doesn't complete the required credits, the consequence will be a failure to move ahead.

It's the same with raising your son. He needs to know that there are consequences for each and every step of his young life. He should be clear on what they are and be held to them daily! He should know that there is a consequence for bad grades, disrespect, being lazy, mistreating females, and so forth. He should also know that his strong, beautiful mother will not waver when it comes to enforcing the consequences. Mothers, this is extremely important and should be a policy within the home. Remember, the best thing you can do for your son as you raise him to be a man is to *hold him accountable as a man.*

Keep in mind that he doesn't have to be 18 or 21 years old to be a man. He can be a man at 13 if you put this message in his heart at an early age. Trust me, I meet a ton of 30, 40, and 50-year-old little boys, and it's a very sad sight. Part of the reason they are that way is because no one ever held them accountable. There is a good chance that their parents didn't enforce the rules of the home. But not your son. Your son will be held accountable, and he will thank you for it later.

In addition to this step, there is one approach you can use that worked wonders for my brothers and me. That's the approach of making life in the home respectfully uncomfortable!

Please let me explain. In short, you don't want your son to

be too comfortable at home. You want to always keep his feet to the fire with a respectful level of discomfort to keep him motivated. For example, when I was coming up, my mother always had a task for us. She always had us doing something. We couldn't just lay around, sleep around, or moan around aimlessly. She found chores, assignments for us to do, in addition to holding us accountable with her policies.

Here is the beauty of her approach. Throughout my childhood, although I was raised in a loving home, I would often say these following words that every man should say:

"I can't wait to get my own house!"

"I can't wait to get my own car!"

"I'm tired of asking my mom for money.
I can't wait to have my own!"

These words should be music to a mother's ears.

You see, although I would be upset while I was saying it as a naïve teenager, the blessing was that my mother was making me just a little uncomfortable in her home so that I could one day have the passion and desire to have my own home. To, one day, be independent and take care of myself.

And that's what you want for your son. You don't want him to be too cozy at your home as if he is at the Ritz Carlton Hotel. You want him to gain a sense of independence so he can be a great provider for the family he will create in the future.

Mothers, please understand you will not harm him by doing this. This will actually be for his great benefit down the road. You don't want him in your back room at 40 years old, waiting for you to cook dinner.

No, no, no. You want your son out of the house as soon as possible and one day, picking you up to take his beautiful mother out to dinner at her favorite restaurant. That's the goal! Please, by all means, mothers. Bless your sons and hold them accountable in every way!

STEP #2: YOUR SON NEEDS TO HAVE A MAN CONVERSATION!

I'm confident that step 2 will be more appealing and is part of the reason you have decided to read this book. Step number 2, I believe, is equally as important or maybe even more important.

Mothers, please hear my heart when I say I absolutely adore the fact of how you can raise a boy into a strong, healthy man. There are many great men who were raised by single mothers. It is clear that there is no task that a mother on a mission can't accomplish.

What I am respectfully suggesting is that you find a man of integrity for your son to have a man-to-man conversation with on a regular basis. This is so important, mothers! Your son needs to know, touch, see, feel, and experience the presence of a man.

He needs to be able to have someone that he can identify his needs with. There are just some things that he will feel more comfortable talking to a man about. He has to have the opportunity to have "the man" conversation.

I frequently think about God's perfect plan of instructing the man to be the head of the home. It always intrigues me how important that role is and how that type of leadership has such a huge impact on the entire family. I believe that God did this for a special reason. When a man of integrity is in the picture, there is a unique type of strength and leadership there. There is both boldness and confidence that can only be given by the Father up above. That being said, it is so important for your son to see that and mimic it as well. Your son needs to experience the presence of a Godly man of integrity!

So, here's what I know. Although they are far few and between, there are still these types of men walking the earth. There are some schoolteachers, basketball coaches, church members, bus drivers, business owners, proud fathers, and many more that pride themselves on adding value to a young man's life. Trust me, mothers, they are out there, and they are ready to be a blessing to your son's life. These are the type of men that don't want anything; they are not looking for a date with you or some other strange request. They simply see a need and are delighted to be of service to you and your son.

Mothers, your son needs you to find these MEN. He might not say it with his words, but he is begging for this direction, and as time goes on, the need becomes greater! Here is the potential danger if you don't: there is a greater chance he will consider learning how to be a man from other sources: TV, school peers, rap videos, gangs, his neighborhood, pornographic movies, or worse. We don't want that for him! We want him to learn the valuable tools as to what it takes to be a man from a man of integrity. But chances are, your son will not make the request.

You have to go and find him.

Mothers, it is my prayer that you will consider these two steps for your son as you raise him to be the man God has called him to be. I am confident that these techniques and philosophies will be of great value to him, as he experiences his journey to manhood.

I MADE A MISTAKE: A MESSAGE TO INCARCERATED MEN

As an international speaker, personal development coach, and now published author, I have had the privilege of traveling the world, helping males of all ages understand what it means to be men of integrity.

Primarily, the majority of my speeches and training are held within US prison systems throughout the entire country. You name it, I have been there. From California to Florida, from state correctional facilities to federal correctional facilities. From large maximum-security prisons for adult males to smaller facilities for young, juvenile offenders. When it comes to the men serving time behind prison walls, I have made a commitment to serve this unique population, and it has been my absolute joy to serve!

During my travels, I have met many men who are full of potential and ready to make a change for the better. It bothers me that some in society think that there are no good men behind prison walls. But I have had an up-close and personal experience, and I can say without a shadow of a doubt that there are many men with an enormous amount of potential. So, to the men that are reading these pages and doing time behind prison walls, I want to leave you with this personal story that has forever change my life:

I was just finishing a speaking engagement at a correctional facility in the state of Iowa. I had the pleasure of speaking to about 200 men that were ready to change for the better and were extremely motivated. When the event ended, I was escorted back to the front of the prison by a man who was doing time there. His name was Mr. James! I have never forgotten how humble he was and how he had a warm and gentle spirit about himself. He spoke with boldness and confidence yet still with care and respect.

We had a great conversation during our commute, but as we arrived at the front of the prison, he said something that would forever change my perception. With great sincerity in his eyes, he said, "Mr. Warren, I made a mistake, but I'm not a mistake!"

WOW! I have to be honest, as a professional speaker myself, I understand and appreciate the value of words. I know how much power words can have on one's life if used correctly. Words can literally be a weapon for greatness and life change. And that's precisely what happened on this very day.

Mr. James' words changed my life with this powerful statement. And here's why! When Mr. James shared these words, it sent my mind into a place that allowed me to examine the difference between the two scenarios.

SCENARIO #1: MAKING A MISTAKE

We all can understand and appreciate the fact that every one that is walking this earth has made not only a few mistakes but many mistakes. We are all guilty of making a poor decision, not thinking before reacting, mistreating someone, not being completely honest, disobeying the rules and regulations of the land, and so forth. I would also argue that it's only the grace of God that we didn't get caught on a few of our mistakes, or we too may be serving time behind prison walls.

But I can only speak for myself.

That being said, a man serving time behind prison walls can acknowledge the fact that we all make mistakes, but "I" got caught, and it's my responsibility as a man to make it right. Making a mistake in life is not necessarily the end of the world, and it can be the start of growing as a man of integrity.

So, with that, making a mistake is just a part of life and not the end-all. There is LIFE after a mistake!

SCENARIO #2 – I AM A MISTAKE

There are many ways a man can take this logic, use it to take him to a dark place, and let it be the philosophy as to which he operates under for the rest of his days. This logic suggests that there is no reason to live. It would sound a little bit like this:

My life is worthless, God made a mistake, my parents should have given me away, my children hate me, society hates me, and last but not least, my time here in prison will lead to nothing.

Even a man who is doing life behind bars may suggest that his life has no purpose, and he is just waiting to die. This is the idea behind I AM a mistake. Let me be crystal clear men...

That logic is a lie!

For every single man behind prison walls who has taken the time to read this book, it is my desire that you adopt the same philosophy as Mr. James. I want you to understand that you made a mistake, which caused you to land in prison, but you are not a mistake and still have many great things inside of you!

God never makes mistakes, and that also includes you. Your life is still worth something, and there is still a great mission for your life. And as a man, it's your job, it's your responsibility, even in prison, to find out what that mission is!

Men, it is with love and respect that I would ask you to cherish these words when I say that you may have made a mistake, but *you are not a mistake!* Your wife needs you. Your children need you. Society needs your gifts and talents. The young man who just got off the bus and has arrived at prison needs your influence and direction. Your mother needs her son to come home a changed man. Your brother and sister are waiting for you to lead the family to greatness.

As you complete this book and finish your time behind the wall, remember this, men, you have a gift that God has placed inside of you, and it was not given so you could waste it away. Tap into that God-given talent and become the great man of integrity He created you to be. It is absolutely impossible for God to make a mistake, men. So, I say this with love in my heart: Let God order your steps!

Go and be great, men!

THE ONLY WAY TO BECOME A MAN

....

"The steps of a good man are
ordered by the Lord!"
-Psalm 37:23

....

What does it mean to be a real man? What does it mean to truly live up to this extraordinary task and operate in this prestigious assignment? How does one learn to function in this capacity with dignity and integrity? What's the one and true way to become a man?

To all of the readers who have taken the time to embrace the words of this book, and to consider these five steps, it has truly been my honor to provide this blueprint that was put on my heart many years ago. It has been a humbling experience serving, speaking, and training under this curriculum and philosophy. It's my hope that all that have taken the time to read this book, let this message sink deep into your heart and use it as a guideline to help you during your journey to manhood and beyond!

The last and the most important message I would like to share is by far the most important message of the text. That message is the one and only true way to become a man. It is with great honor and respect to share with you that the only true way to become a man is:

"Trust in the Lord with all your heart and lean not on your own understanding. In all your ways submit to him, and he will make your paths straight."

-Proverbs 3:5-6

Men, this book covered a variety of things from my personal life story, the five-step curriculum, and action steps that you can use to help you on your journey to manhood. But none of that is more important than making God the top priority of your life. *This is the only way to become a MAN.*

The truth of the matter is that unless you take this ultimate step, everything else will be a waste of time. Walking this earth without direction will ultimately lead you to a place of confusion, misdirection, fear, wasted time, and a life without a purpose. This is why this is the most important step in any man's life. There comes a time when a man has to surrender his life to God and allow him to order his steps in all that he does. This means trusting him to guide you in choosing a career, choosing a spouse, managing finances, serving the community, and telling others about God's love.

Men, becoming a MAN must be earned and learned. You earn the right to be called a MAN when you decide to live a life of integrity, but you learn how to be a man by the most powerful man of all, God the father!

HERE IS A BONUS

As you finish this book and start your new journey to manhood, I would like you to consider these three things in addition to everything we have discussed. I like to call them the three "P's": Every man must be the *Pastor, Protector,* and *Provider* of their home. Let's take a quick look at a breakdown of each one.

Pastor: No matter if you are a religious person or not, every home is operating under some type of family law, rules, or policy that everyone must agree to. An example of this would be, no profanity, no cheating, no lying, always show respect, always encourage one another, keep the house clean, and so on. But where does this come from? Who makes the rules, and who should be enforcing them? It's very simple.

God makes the rules, and it's the man's job to enforce them. That being said, the only way to know God's rules that should be enforced in the home is to spend time with Him and study His word. Once you commit to this, you will now be equipped to be the Pastor of your home. Your wife and children should be able to come to you and receive Godly wisdom.

So, make it a priority to seek God and lead your family in a godly way. This will be the best foundation you can set as you lead your family as the man of the home.

Protector: I'm sure when you hear this word, you may be thinking of physical strength or something of that nature and you would be correct. But this role actually means a little bit more. As the protector of the home, the man's job is to ensure that no one mistreats, misuses, abuses, disrespects, or violates the family in any way. God has given us a strong frame to handle this in the physical, so, we should always be ready in the event our family is challenged in that way.

But what about the emotional? Yes, as a man, it is your job to protect your family's heart as well. They should feel secure in knowing that you will never leave them nor mistreat them in any way. Your spouse should know she can depend on you and you are interested in her feelings. Your children should know that they can come to their father without any shame.

That being said, as the man of the home, it's your job to protect the family from all physical harm as well as emotional harm. Your family needs your protection from all of the above!

Provider: Okay, Men, let's not make this too dramatic. I don't want to give any magical or fantastical statement regarding this role. I'd rather just be as black and white as possible. Men, you have to work! There is no other way to put it. As the man of the home, it is your responsibility – not your wife's – to provide shelter, food, clothes, transportation, electricity, running water, entertainment, and any other necessity for the family. It's your job to provide these things, men, and remember to be delighted to do it (step #4).

Men, if your wife decides to work as well, that is just an added bonus, but it is not a requirement for her. This should always be an option. For you as the man of the home, you don't have that option, Sir; your family is ultimately depending on you to provide.

No excuses!

Now, to all who have read these words, you are equipped to serve the rest of your days as the man of the home and as a godly man of integrity. The success of your family and community depends on you making this transition.

You are MAN enough for the job!

Helping "Males" Become "Men"

Baron Warren believes that "MALES" have to make a conscious decision to put away childish things and earn the right to be called a "MAN." His passionate speaking style and his tough-love approach has motivated, inspired, and influenced many men around the country and beyond.

Baron served proudly in the United States Navy for a total of eight years, during a time of war following the attacks on 9/11. While on active duty, Baron traveled to over twenty different countries worldwide and stayed deployed out to sea for up to eight months at a time.

Baron received his Bachelor's Degree in Psychology from the University of La Verne in Southern California in 2012 and was honorably discharged from the military that same year. Upon leaving the military, Baron served as a correctional officer for several years with the Michigan Department of Corrections and conducted group training involving conflict resolution and living a life of integrity with hundreds of prisoners statewide.

Baron is currently the president of Cuts & Coaching LLC, which serves males in the area of education, employment, independent living, and grooming standards for daily life.

Baron Warren has dedicated his life to serving his community by making a positive impact on those in need.

For more information, please visit:
www.cutsandcoaching.com
www.baronwarren.com

Made in USA - Kendallville, IN
1085539_9780578638188
04.22.2020 0748